SCHOLASTIC

Grades 2–3

ACTIVITIES FOR
FAST FINISHERS
MATH

55 Reproducible Puzzles, Brain Teasers, and Other Independent, Learning-Rich Activities Kids Can't Resist!

by Jan Meyer

New York • Toronto • London • Auckland • Sydney
Mexico City • New Delhi • Hong Kong • Buenos Aires

Teaching *Resources*

FOR DAVID, LYNDSEY, AND DYLAN

Editor: Mela Ottaiano
Cover design: Brian LaRossa
Interior design: Melinda Belter
Interior illustrations: Teresa Anderko

ISBN-13: 978-0-545-15984-5
ISBN-10: 0-545-15984-9

2 3 4 5 6 7 8 9 10   40   17 16 15 14 13 12 11 10

TABLE OF CONTENTS

ABOUT THIS BOOK

Teachers frequently ask, "What, other than silent reading, can I use to keep fast finishers productively busy?" This book has been designed to address this concern.

- There are 55 pages of engaging math activities.
- Fast finishers can work on these activities independently.
- A relatively short period of time is required to complete most of these pages.

The activities in this book cover topics you teach in your classroom: computation, problem solving, and a wide variety of specific math skills. They provide practice with place value, rounding numbers, skip counting, addition, subtraction, multiplication, fractions, measurement, time, money, graphs, story problems, and more. You'll also find a large section of fun puzzle activities that stimulate an interest in playing with numbers. Not your ordinary fill-in-the-blanks exercises, these 55 pages include a maze, cross-number puzzles, magic paths, number riddles to solve, amazing facts, magic squares, a sudoku puzzle, and a broad array of other child-pleasing activities.

Students of varying abilities can enjoy these activities. For those who need help with certain skill areas, some pages have examples and/or a special "handy hints" section. For students with high-level skills, a number of pages include a "Bonus!" activity for an added challenge.

They've Disappeared!

Five numbers have disappeared from each of these puzzle boxes. Can you figure out which five are missing?

Hint
It helps to check off the numbers as you find them.

1. These numbers increase by three. They start at 3 and end at 69.

48	54	24	6	9	39
66	69	12	3	21	60
36	27	15	45	63	33

The missing numbers are

_____ .

2. These numbers decrease by two. They start at 89 and end at 47.

89	63	49	61	77	53
73	55	83	47	85
79	65	69	57	87	71

The missing numbers are

_____ .

3. These numbers decrease by five. They start at 95 and end at 5.

25	70	10	85	60
55	30	20	45	80
95	5	50	90

The missing numbers are

_____ .

4. These numbers increase by two. They start at 75 and end at 115.

81	93	103	75	115	97
91	107	105	89	109
83	77	85	113	95

The missing numbers are

_____ .

Name _____

Date _____

Skip Counting Caterpillars

Each of these caterpillars is skip counting by a different number. Can you figure out what each one is counting by? Fill in the numbers that they have missed.

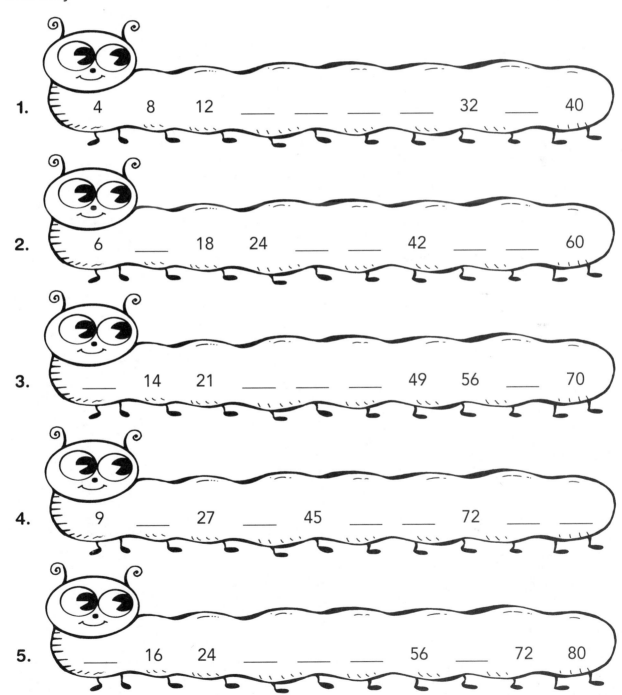

1. 4   8   12   ___   ___   ___   32   ___   40

2. 6   ___   18   24   ___   42   ___   ___   60

3. ___   14   21   ___   ___   ___   49   56   ___   70

4. 9   ___   27   ___   45   ___   72   ___   ___

5. ___   16   24   ___   ___   56   ___   72   80

Fill 'Em In

There are missing parts in each of these patterns of numbers, letters, and designs. Can you figure out what's missing and fill them in? Fill in what's missing in each of these patterns.

1. ABC   BCD   _____   DEF   _____   FGH   GHI

2. 15   16   25   ____   35   36   45   46   ____   56   65   66

3. ▲   _____   ▲▲   ✖✖   ▲▲▲   ✖✖✖   _____   ✖✖✖✖

4. 99   88   77   ____   55   ____   33   22   11

5. a   c   e   g   i   ___   m   ___   q   s   u   w

6. ⬇   ➡   ⬆   ⬅   ⬇   ____   ⬆   ⬅   ⬇   ➡   ___   ⬅

7. z   y   ___   w   v   u   ___   s   r   q   ___   o

8. A   Z   ___   Y   C   X   D   ___   E   V   ___   U   G

⭐ **Bonus!**   Make up your own pattern using letters or designs.

Activities for Fast Finishers: Math © 2010 by Jan Meyer, Scholastic Teaching Resources

Name _____

Date _____

Number-Pattern Parades

Can you figure out the pattern for each of these series? What number comes next? Fill in the next number in the box at the end of each of pattern.

1. 20   40   60   80   100   120   140   160   180   [ ]

2. 4   40   400   4,000   40,000   [ ]

3. 1   2   2   3   3   3   4   4   4   4   5   5   5   5   [ ]

4. 21   12   32   23   43   34   54   [ ]

5. 33 – 11 = 22   32 – 10 = 22   31 – 9 = 22   [ ]

6. 14 + 5 = 19   13 + 6 = 19   12 + 7 = 19   [ ]

Bonus! What comes next in each of these patterns?

EXAMPLE: 3   1   4   2   5   3   6
                    -2 $+3$ -2 $+3$ -2 $+3$

a. 1   2   4   7   11   16   [ ]

b. 3   2   6   5   9   8   12   11   [ ]

Hint

Look at the relationship between each number and the number that follows it in the series.

How Amazing!

Read the amazing facts below. Then follow the directions to round each number.

1. The anaconda is one of the world's largest snakes. Adult male anacondas at least 26 feet long have been seen. Round that number to the nearest ten. _____

2. The highest mountain in the United States is Mount McKinley. It is 20,320 feet high. Round that number to the nearest hundred. _____

3. One of the longest wooden roller coasters in the United States is in Ohio. It is called "Mean Streak" and is 5,427 feet long. Round that number to the nearest thousand. _____

4. A new stadium for the New York Yankees was finished in 2009. It has 50,086 seats. Round that number to the nearest hundred. _____.

RULES FOR ROUNDING

Look at the number to the right of the number in the place you are rounding to.
* If it is 4 or less, the number in the place you are rounding to remains the same.
* If it is 5 or more, the number in the place you are rounding to increases by 1.
All of the numbers to the right of the place you are rounding to become 0.

• EXAMPLES •

523 rounded to the nearest ten is 520.
1,482 rounded to the nearest hundred is 1,500.

Activities for Fast Finishers: Math © 2010 by Jan Meyer, Scholastic Teaching Resources

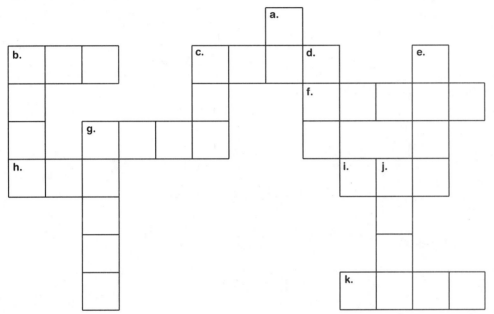

Name _____

Date _____

Cross-Number Puzzle 1

Here's a chance to practice your place-value skills. Fill in the numbers that match the place-value definitions. Read each puzzle clue carefully.

Hint

The place value clues may not go in order from highest to lowest place.

Across

b. seven hundreds, five tens, and six ones

c. three thousands, nine tens, zero hundreds, and nine ones

f. sixty thousands, two tens, seven ones, and five hundreds

g. six hundreds, seven thousands, two tens, and nine ones

h. zero ones, five hundreds, and one ten

i. five hundreds, seven tens, and eight ones

k. zero hundreds, two ones, six tens, and five thousands

Down

a. nine ones and eight tens

b. seven thousands, three hundreds, four tens, and five ones

c. nine ones, three hundreds, and two tens

d. nine hundreds, six tens, and zero ones

e. two hundreds, eight ones, six tens, and one thousand

g. seventy thousands, four ones, eight hundreds, and six tens

j. zero ones, zero hundreds, seven thousands, and seven tens

Any Old Place Won't Do

Draw a line from a place value in the left column to a number in the right column that has a digit with that place value.

1. four tens   **a.** 11,708

2. eight ten thousands   **b.** 748,910

3. nine hundreds   **c.** 30,246

4. five ones   **d.** 14,861

5. eight hundred thousands   **e.** 426,379

6. six tens   **f.** 81,392

7. seven thousands   **g.** 917,573

8. zero ten thousands   **h.** 2,685

9. seven hundreds   **i.** 908,839

10. four hundred thousands   **j.** 869,554

Bonus! What is the largest number in the right column? _____

PLACE VALUE

Here are the place values for the number 659,432.

hundred thousands	ten thousands	thousands	hundreds	tens	ones
6	5	9	4	3	2

Activities for Fast Finishers: Math © 2010 by Jan Meyer, Scholastic Teaching Resources

Puzzlers

Read the clues and then answer the questions.

1. What is the greatest five-digit number you can make with the digits 1, 0, 9, 0, and 2? _____

2. What two different odd numbers between 0 and 10 add up to 16? _____

3. What is the greatest number with 3 digits? _____

4. Rearrange the digits in the number 403 so that when you multiply it by 2, the product is 608. The rearranged number is _____ .

5. The product of these two numbers is 12. Their difference is 1. What is their sum? _____

6. What do these four subtraction problems have in common: 16 – 9, 15 – 8, 87 – 80, and 12 – 5? _____

_____

Bonus! What four-digit numbers can you make with the digits 3, 2, 3, and 3?

_____ _____

_____ _____

Even More Puzzling Puzzlers

Read the clues and then answer the questions.

1. Rearrange the digits in the number 234 so that when you multiply it by 3, the product is 1,269. The rearranged number is _____ .

2. Double 20. Double the results. What number do you have to subtract to get back to 20? _____

3. The product of these two numbers is 36. Their sum is 12. What is their difference? _____

4. What's the smallest six digit number you can make with the digits 6, 8, 1, 3, 1, 4? _____

5. Add all the even numbers below 12. What is the result? _____

6. When you multiply me by 5 you get 40. What do you get when you divide me by 2? _____

7. If you write the numbers between 1 and 40, how many 3's will you write? _____

8. What number between 1 and 10 has the same value as the number of letters in its name? _____

Bonus! What do these three numbers have in common: 29, 614, and 38? _____

Activities for Fast Finishers: Math © 2010 by Jan Meyer, Scholastic Teaching Resources

Name _____

Date _____

Number Riddles

Read all of the clues carefully. Then answer the questions.

1. When you subtract me from 20, the difference is 14. When you multiply me by 6, the product is 36. What number am I? _____

2. I'm a two-digit number between 0 and 30. My two digits add up to 1. What number am I? _____

3. I'm an odd three-digit number. I'm greater than 95 and less than 102. What number am I? _____

4. One of my addends is 10. My other addend is ½ of 10. What number am I? _____

5. When you multiply me by 6, the product is 30. When you add me to 77, the sum is 82. What number am I? _____

6. I'm a four-digit number and all of my digits are the same. The sum of my digits is 12. What number am I? _____

7. I'm an even number between 70 and 90. The sum of my two digits is 16. What number am I? _____

Bonus! Make up a number riddle to try on your classmates.

_____

_____

_____

Activities for Fast Finishers: Math © 2010 by Jan Meyer, Scholastic Teaching Resources

Name _____

Date _____

More Number Riddles

Read all of the clues carefully. Then answer the questions.

1. I'm a two-digit number between 30 and 40. My two digits add up to 6. What number am I? _____

2. I'm a three-digit number. My ones digit is 2. My hundreds digit is 7. My tens digit is the difference between my hundreds digit and my ones digit. What number am I? _____

3. When you add me to 17, the sum is 26. When you multiply me by 4, the product is 36. What number am I? _____

4. I am greater than the sum of 37 + 8 and less than the product of 6 x 8. I'm definitely odd. What number am I? _____

5. I'm a three-digit number and my digits are all the same. The sum of my digits is 24. What number am I? _____

6. When you subtract me from 44, my difference is 20. When you double me, the result is 48. What number am I? _____

7. I'm a number between 55 and 65. The sum of my digits is 7. What number am I? _____

8. I'm an even number between 450 and 500. My ones digit is 2. My tens digit is 4 times my ones digit. What number am I? _____

Bonus! One of my factors is 6. The other is of ⅓ that. What number am I? _____

Activities for Fast Finishers: Math © 2010 by Jan Meyer, Scholastic Teaching Resources

Name _____

Date _____

Meet the Slammers

Here is a picture of the Slammers, the best baseball team in the South Lakes junior league. This year, they won all but one of their games. Use the picture to answer these questions.

1. What fraction of the Slammers are wearing shirts with short sleeves?

_____

2. What fraction of the Slammers are wearing glasses? _____

3. What fraction of the Slammers are standing? _____

4. What fraction of the Slammers are girls? _____

5. What fraction of the Slammers are boys? _____

6. What fraction of the girls have curly hair? _____

7. What fraction of the boys are wearing baseball caps. _____

8. What fraction of the boys who are wearing baseball caps are holding baseball bats? _____

Bonus! One-third of the Slammers have pet dogs at home. How many Slammers is that? _____

Name _____

Date _____

A Fair Share

Read each problem. Then draw in the boxes to help you solve the problems.

1. Mr. Bates caught 12 fish. He wants to divide them equally between himself and his friend. Draw the fish in the box and then divide them into 2 equal groups by circling each group.
How many fish did his friend get? _____

2. Mrs. Chu found 9 shiny stones at the beach. She wants to divide them equally and give ⅓ to each of her 3 daughters. Draw the stones in the box and then divide them into 3 equal groups by circling each group.
How many stones did each daughter get? _____

3. Aunt Rosie picked 20 flowers in her garden. She wants to keep ⅘ of the flowers for herself and give ⅕ of them to her neighbor. Draw the flowers in the box and then divide them into 5 equal groups by circling each group.
How many flowers did Aunt Rosie keep for herself? _____
How many flowers will her neighbor get? _____

Activities for Fast Finishers: Math © 2010 by Jan Meyer, Scholastic Teaching Resources

Name _____

Date _____

To the Top

Can you add your way to the top of these towers? Add each pair of side-by-side numbers together. Write their sum in the box directly above the pair. Continue to add each pair until you reach the top of the tower.

EXAMPLE:

```
        14
      8    6  ---- 8 + 6 = 14
3 + 5 = 8 ---- 3   5   1  ---- 5 + 1 = 6
```

1.

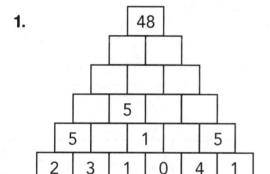

2.

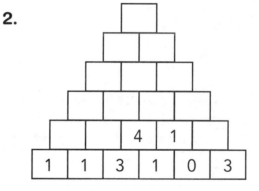

3.

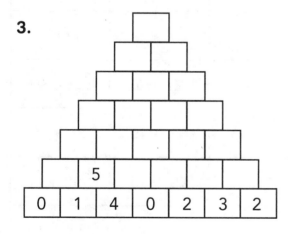

4.

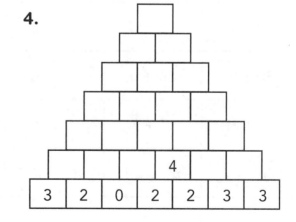

Name _____

Date _____

Cheese, Please

Can you help this little mouse find its way through the maze of equations to reach the cheese? To get from the start of the maze to the end of the maze, shade in only those boxes with equations that have a sum that is even. You may move across (→), down (↓), or diagonally (↘).

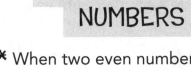

ODD AND EVEN NUMBERS

* When two even numbers are added, the sum is always even.

* When an even number and an odd number are added, the sum is always odd.

* When two odd numbers are added, the sum is always even.

Start

$20 + 2$	$9 + 10$	$5 + 4$	$18 + 3$	$35 + 5$	$4 + 9$
$44 + 6$	$22 + 15$	$41 + 8$	$62 + 8$	$34 + 17$	$28 + 2$
$13 + 1$	$43 + 3$	$66 + 5$	$33 + 1$	$44 + 9$	$52 + 6$
$52 + 3$	$38 + 6$	$88 + 11$	$12 + 4$	$27 + 6$	$21 + 9$
$39 + 22$	$17 + 7$	$8 + 2$	$10 + 53$	$62 + 45$	$55 + 11$
$71 + 24$	$55 + 34$	$28 + 19$	$82 + 17$	$29 + 36$	$99 + 1$

Finish

Activities for Fast Finishers: Math © 2010 by Jan Meyer, Scholastic Teaching Resources

The Sign Snatcher

Snarg the sign snatcher has taken away the plus and minus signs from each of these equations. Can you put the correct ones back in? Put a plus or a minus sign in each of the boxes.

· EXAMPLE ·

$15 \square 5 \square 1 = 11$ ➡ $15 \boxed{-} 5 \boxed{+} 1 = 11$

1. $5 \square 5 \square 10 = 20$

2. $7 \square 2 \square 10 = 19$

3. $8 \square 3 \square 5 = 10$

4. $16 \square 1 \square 2 = 13$

5. $100 \square 100 \square 50 = 50$

6. $42 \square 4 \square 2 = 48$

7. $78 \square 2 \square 10 = 70$

8. $15 \square 3 \square 2 = 14$

Hint

Check your answers by trying the equations after you've put in the signs.

Bonus! Now try this even more challenging equation.

$330 \square 110 \square 4 = 224$

Activities for Fast Finishers: Math © 2010 by Jan Meyer, Scholastic Teaching Resources

Name _____

Date _____

Legs and Toes

Read the problems and then use multiplication to answer the questions.

1. An owl has a total of 8 toes. How many toes do 5 owls have?

_____

2. A mosquito, like most insects, has 6 legs. How many legs do 6 mosquitoes have? _____

3. A hippo has 4 toes on each foot. How many toes does a hippo have in all? _____

4. A spider has 8 legs. How many legs do 4 spiders have?

_____

5. An ostrich has a total of 4 toes. How many toes do 20 ostriches have? _____

6. A porcupine has 5 toes on each of its front paws and 4 toes on each of its back paws. How many toes does a porcupine have in all? _____

Bonus! Which has more toes: 2 owls or 3 ostriches? _____

Activities for Fast Finishers: Math © 2010 by Jan Meyer, Scholastic Teaching Resources

That's Really Odd!

In each row, circle the pairs of numbers next to each other that have a sum that is odd. For example, at the beginning of the first row, the 17 and 3, the 3 and 5, and the 5 and 11 should not be circled because 17 + 3 = 20, 3 + 5 = 8, and 5 + 11 = 16. The 11 and 2 should be circled because 11 + 2 = 13.

1.	17	3	5	11	2	18	6	8	1	17
2.	7	7	5	16	4	27	3	18	4	7
3.	25	25	50	30	22	12	13	11	5	9
4.	8	8	4	16	15	5	25	10	6	9
5.	33	6	14	15	15	2	28	4	40	50
6.	1	9	9	7	11	9	12	8	15	7

In each row, circle the pairs of numbers next to each other that have a product that is odd. For example, at the beginning of the first row, the 6 and 1 should not be circled because 6 x 1 = 6. The 1 and 5 should be circled because 1 x 5 = 5.

7.	6	1	5	2	3	3	4	5	5	2
8.	9	2	9	3	6	6	1	7	2	11
9.	7	3	8	5	7	4	4	3	5	4
10.	4	9	5	6	7	3	2	5	9	2
11.	3	1	8	4	1	13	2	10	5	3
12.	11	5	6	7	7	2	12	3	13	2

Name _____

Date _____

Roxie's Front-End Repairs

Missing the front end of an arithmetic problem? Go to Roxie's. She has the best front-end repair shop in town! Look in Roxie's box of spare parts for the correct front end for each of these equations. When you find it, write it on the line in front of the problem where it belongs. Be careful, though. You won't need all of Roxie's spare parts.

1. _____ 8 = 40

2. _____ 11 = 22

3. _____ 3 = 27

4. _____ 8 = 20

5. _____ 6 = 23

6. _____ 12 = 27

7. _____ 3 = 21

8. _____ 6 = 24

9. _____ 15 = 21

10. _____ 6 = 36

SPARE PARTS

14 +

6 +

4 ×

31 +

12 +

8 ×

9 ×

39 –

26 –

5 ×

11 +

7 ×

23 +

6 ×

28 –

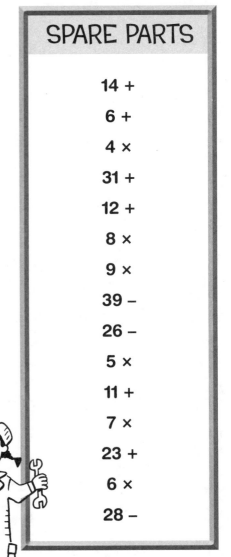

Name _____

Date _____

Math Paths

Make your way along these paths by adding, subtracting, or multiplying as required. Fill in the missing numbers on each of these paths by solving each equation as you move forward.

· EXAMPLE ·

3 – 2 ☐ + 5 ☐ × 2 ☐ – 3 ☐ ➡ 3 – 2 [1] + 5 [6] × 2 [12] – 3 [9]

1. 8 – 2 ☐ × 2 ☐ – 9 ☐ + 8 ☐ – 7 ☐ × 5 ☐ – 6 ☐

2. 29 – 15 ☐ + 4 ☐ + 2 ☐ × 3 ☐ – 50 ☐ – 1 ☐ × 2 ☐

3. 20 – 0 ☐ + 13 ☐ × 2 ☐ – 45 ☐ + 9 ☐ – 27 ☐ × 4 ☐

4. 5 × 3 ☐ – 8 ☐ × 2 ☐ + 55 ☐ + 3 ☐ – 60 ☐ × 2 ☐

Fast Finishers

ADDITION, SUBTRACTION & MULTIPLICATION

How Many Is That?

To solve these problems, you need to provide the numbers. Read the clues, figure out the numbers, and solve the problems.

1. Multiply the number of states in the United States by the number of horns on a bull. What's the product? _____

2. Subtract the number of bases on a baseball field from the number of letters in the alphabet. What's the difference? _____

3. Add the number of days in most years to the number of seasons. What's the sum? _____

4. Subtract the number of arms on an octopus from the number of sides on an octagon. What's the difference? _____

5. Multiply the number of children in a set of twins by the number of wheels on a tricycle. What's the product? _____

6. Subtract the number of eggs in a dozen from the number of hours in a day. What's the difference? _____

Bonus! Multiply the number of legs on a snake by the number of states in the U.S. What's the product? _____

Fast Finishers

Name _____

Date _____

ADDITION, SUBTRACTION &
MULTIPLICATION

Cross-Number Puzzle 2

Fill in the missing numbers for each of the equations in the rows going across and the columns going down.

a.4	x		=	1	b.2		c.6			d.9	9	–			=	e.1
0				f.8	x		=	4	0	+						5
x				+				–								–
g.2	x	h.	=	1	2		i.	x	1	1	=	4	4			
=		x		=					1							=
3		3					=		j.6	k.4	+			=	8	l.8
		=					2			x						3
1		1		m.	x	2	=	1	4							+
n.	+	8	1	=	9	0				=						
										1						=
									o.6	0	–			=	9	
																2

Across

a. 4 × ___ = 12

d. 99 – ___ ___ = 1

f. 8 × ___ = 40

g. 2 × ___ = 12

i. ___ × 11 = 44

j. 64 + ___ ___ = 88

m. ___ × 2 = 14

n. ___ + 81 = 90

o. 60 – ___ ___ = 9

Down

a. 40 × 2 = ___ ___

b. 28 + 2 = ___ ___

c. 64 – ___ ___ = 22

d. 9 + ___ = 16

e. 15 – ___ = 8

h. ___ × 3 = 18

k. 4 × ___ = 16

l. 83 + ___ = 92

Three in a Row

In each puzzle, there are three number problems in a row that all have the same answer. Find the correct row and draw a line through it. The row can go across, down, or diagonally.

Hint

You may want to put the answer by each problem and then decide where to draw the line.

1. Find three addition problems in a row with the same answer.

18 + 7	20 + 5	14 + 12
9 + 16	19 + 6	12 + 12
14 + 11	6 + 17	21 + 3

2. Find three subtraction problems in a row with the same difference.

35 – 11	77 – 53	25 – 13
66 – 42	44 – 32	38 – 26
18 – 6	20 – 7	22 – 9

3. Find three multiplication problems in a row with the same answer.

15 × 2	3 × 10	12 × 2
30 × 1	5 × 6	2 × 14
4 × 6	3 × 8	24 × 1

4. Find three number problems in a row with the same answer.

6 x 3	21 – 3	9 + 8
11 + 7	9 x 2	29 – 12
5 × 4	18 + 2	38 – 18

Bonus! Make up a Three in a Row math problem for a classmate to try.

Activities for Fast Finishers: Math © 2010 by Jan Meyer, Scholastic Teaching Resources

Name _____

Date _____

ADDITION, SUBTRACTION &
MULTIPLICATION

Tic Tac Total

In each of these puzzles, draw a line through the row that has three equations that could each (by adding, subtracting, or multiplying) equal the number in the starburst above the puzzle. Then put the correct operation sign (+, –, or x) in each box between the numbers in the row through which you drew the line. The correct row can go across, down, or diagonally.

1. 12

6 ☐ 5	4 ☐ 3	16 ☐ 3
2 ☐ 8	11 ☐ 1	5 ☐ 3
7 ☐ 4	8 ☐ 4	2 ☐ 7

2. 16

4 ☐ 4	7 ☐ 3	8 ☐ 9
5 ☐ 3	19 ☐ 3	6 ☐ 9
6 ☐ 4	12 ☐ 5	2 ☐ 8

3. 21

5 ☐ 4	19 ☐ 3	7 ☐ 3
11 ☐ 2	7 ☐ 4	22 ☐ 1
39 ☐ 8	11 ☐ 9	17 ☐ 4

4. 24

29 ☐ 4	9 ☐ 2	6 ☐ 6
19 ☐ 4	15 ☐ 8	7 ☐ 16
6 ☐ 4	8 ☐ 3	2 ☐ 12

Bonus! Make up a Tic Tac Total math problem for a classmate to try.

The Time Machine

The time machine has taken you back more than 2,000 years. You are living in ancient Rome. Can you solve these Roman numeral problems? Write your answers in Roman numerals.

ROMAN NUMERALS

Here are the Roman numerals for the numbers 1 through 20.

I = 1	XI = 11
II = 2	XII = 12
III = 3	XIII = 13
IV = 4	XIV = 14
V = 5	XV = 15
VI = 6	XVI = 16
VII = 7	XVII = 17
VIII = 8	XVIII = 18
IX = 9	XIX = 19
X = 10	XX = 20

EXAMPLE: V + V = X

1. III + II = _____

2. XI + V = _____

3. VIII – II = _____

4. IX – V = _____

5. VI + VIII = _____

6. XI – X = _____

7. XV + V = _____

8. X – IV = _____

9. XII + VII = _____

10. XX – II = _____

11. IV + XI = _____

12. XX – I = _____

Bonus!

a. What do you think is the Roman numeral for 29? _____

b. What do you think is the Roman numeral for 30? _____

c. What do you think is the Roman numeral for 38? _____

Name _____

Date _____

Tell Me More

Sometimes not enough information is given to solve a story problem. Read each story problem. Then write down what else you need to know in order to solve the problem.

1. The town pool was filled with children. One half of the children in the pool were boys and the other half were girls. How many of the children in the pool were girls? _____

_____

2. Jillian's mother bought 2 hotdogs for each person who was coming to the cookout. How many hotdogs did she buy? _____

_____

3. The population of Lost Hope was 56. One family just moved to the city. What is the population of Lost Hope now? _____

_____

4. Tarik works after school 5 days each week. If he earns the same amount of money each day, how much can he earn in 3 weeks? _____

_____

5. Ginger spent $30 for new shoes and $4 for new socks. How much money did she have left? _____

_____

More Than Enough

These story problems have more information than is needed to solve them. Cross out the information that isn't needed and then solve the problem.

1. Kevin is growing tomatoes in his garden. He has 5 rows of plants with 4 plants in each row. Yesterday, he picked 9 tomatoes. Today he picked 3 tomatoes. How many tomato plants does Kevin have?

   _____

2. Carmela has won 12 medals for back dives and 6 medals for dives off the high board. She practices diving for 2 hours each day and always practices 5 days a week. How many medals for diving has Carmela won?

   _____

3. Shoji lives 5 miles from his school. He lives 2 miles from the park. If he rides his bike from his home to the park and then back to his home, how many miles in all will he ride? _____

4. Shay brought in a tray with 12 brownies on it. Each brownie had 4 walnuts in it. Shay's 4 friends each ate 2 brownies. If Shay also ate 2 brownies, how many brownies were left on the tray? _____

5. At Sid's Cycle Shop it costs $8 an hour to rent a bike. On Sunday, the shop rented 70 bikes and made about $3,000 for the day. How much does it cost to rent a bike for 4 hours? _____

Name _____

Date _____

Looking for Clues

Each of these story problems has a small group of words that are clues to whether you need to use addition or subtraction to solve the problem. Circle the word clues in each problem. Then write the math operation you'll use and the answer to the problem.

EXAMPLE: Mrs. Robertson bought 20 hot dogs and 24 hot dog buns for the picnic. How many more hot dog buns than hot dogs did she buy?

Math operation: _Subtraction_   **Answer:** _4_

1. At Roadrunner Ranch you can have a two-hour horseback ride for $15.00 or a one-hour horseback ride for $9.00. What is the difference in cost between a two-hour and a one-hour horseback ride?

Math operation: _____   **Answer:** _____

2. The Wildcats had 15 hits in their first game, 12 hits in their second game, and 23 hits in their third game. How many hits did they have in all in these three games? **Math operation:** _____   **Answer:** _____

3. Harriet Hippo weighs 2,255 pounds. Romeo Rhino weighs 2,005 pounds. How much less does Romeo Rhino weigh?

Math operation: _____   **Answer:** _____

4. While hiking in the woods, Meg saw 6 deer, 15 squirrels, 5 chipmunks, and 2 porcupines. What is the total number of animals she saw?

Math operation: _____   **Answer:** _____

Bonus! Make up an addition or a subtraction story problem in which you use at least one clue word.

Name _____

Date _____

Picture It

Drawing a picture can sometimes help in solving story problems. Try this strategy to help solve these story problems. First complete the picture, and then solve the problem.

EXAMPLE: Monica wants to give 3 candy hearts to 5 of her friends for Valentine's Day. How many candy hearts does she need?

Answer: _3 x 5 = 15 candy hearts_

1. Mia put a total of 24 marbles in 4 small boxes. She put 6 marbles in the first box, 5 in the second box, and 7 in the third box. How many marbles did she put in the fourth box?

Answer: _____

2. Hillary makes beaded bracelets. She uses 8 beads for each bracelet. How many complete bracelets can she make with 30 beads?

Answer: _____

3. Jake ate 12 peanuts. Gary ate ½ as many peanuts as Jake. Peter ate twice as many peanuts as Gary. How many peanuts did these boys eat in all?

Answer: _____

Jake	Gary	Peter

Activities for Fast Finishers: Math © 2010 by Jan Meyer, Scholastic Teaching Resources

Name _____

Date _____

Put It in a Chart

Using a chart is sometimes helpful in solving difficult story problems. Try this strategy to help solve a puzzling story problem.

EXAMPLE: Aiko, Candace, and Hannah each have a different favorite dessert. One likes chocolate cake best, one likes apple pie best, and one likes chocolate ice cream best. Candace does not like chocolate. Hannah only likes desserts that are cold. What is each girl's favorite dessert?

CHART

	AIKO	CANDACE	HANNAH
chocolate cake	(yes)	no	no
apple pie		(yes)	no
chocolate ice cream		no	(yes)

EXPLANATION: Since Candace doesn't like chocolate, apple pie must be her favorite. Since Hannah only likes cold desserts, chocolate ice cream must be her favorite. That leaves chocolate cake. So that must be Aiko's favorite.

Is This Your Pet?

Scott, Mark, Zack, and Carla each have a different pet. One has a lizard, one has a puppy, one has a snake, and one has a bird. Zack doesn't like reptiles. Mark doesn't like pets with legs. Carla's pet can walk on two legs. What kind of pet does each one have?

	SCOTT	MARK	ZACK	CARLA
lizard				
puppy				
snake				
bird				

Scott has a _____   Mark has a _____

Zack has a _____   Carla has a _____

Who Wants Chocolate?

Super Scoops wants to know how popular each of its ice cream flavors is. Can you help them figure it out? Here is what they sold one day:

ICE CREAM FLAVOR	NUMBER OF PINTS SOLD
Raspberry Ripple	10
Caramel Crunch	20
Mint Chip	10
Vanilla	8
Nutty Double Fudge	40
Strawberry Swirl	12

1. What was their most popular flavor? _____

2. What was their least popular flavor? _____

3. How many pints of Caramel Crunch did they sell? _____

4. What two flavors sold the same number of pints?

   _____ and _____

5. How many pints of Raspberry Ripple and Strawberry Swirl did they

   sell in total? _____

6. How many more pints of Strawberry Swirl than Mint Chip did

   they sell? _____

7. How many pints in all did they sell? _____

8. What flavor would you buy? _____

Activities for Fast Finishers: Math © 2010 by Jan Meyer, Scholastic Teaching Resources

Batter Up

The Cedarville Sluggers are a winning baseball team. The table shows last season's number of hits for their best batters. First, add up each of the batter's hits and fill in the "Total Hits" column. Then answer the questions.

PLAYER	SINGLES	DOUBLES	TRIPLES	HOMERUNS	TOTAL HITS
Gene Rosen	53	6	0	3	
Roberto Lopez	68	3	2	5	
Matt Branford	48	2	0	2	
Montel Clark	61	5	3	0	
Steve Williams	75	6	1	4	
Vince Nathan	59	4	0	1	

1. Which of these players has the greatest number of singles? _____

2. Who has more doubles and triples combined: Steve Williams or

   Montel Clark? _____

3. How many homeruns did these players hit in all? _____

4. How many more singles did Steve Williams hit than Vince Nathan hit?

   _____

5. Which of these players had the greatest number of hits? _____

6. How many doubles did these players hit in all? _____

Bonus! Which player has the fewest doubles, triples, and

homeruns combined? _____

Activities for Fast Finishers: Math © 2010 by Jan Meyer, Scholastic Teaching Resources

Norton's Novelties

Norton's Novelty Shop sells tricks that make people laugh and scream. Norton has made a graph to show this weekend's sales for five of his popular novelties. Use his line graph to answer the questions below.

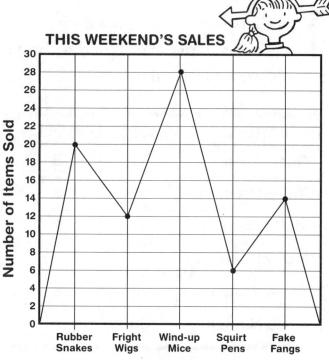

THIS WEEKEND'S SALES

Number of Items Sold

Popular Novelties: Rubber Snakes, Fright Wigs, Wind-up Mice, Squirt Pens, Fake Fangs

1. How many fright wigs did he sell? _____

2. Which of his novelties sold the best that weekend? _____

3. Which of his novelties had the fewest sales that weekend? _____

4. How many fright wigs and wind-up mice did he sell in all? _____

5. Which had more sales: fake fangs or rubber snakes? _____

6. How many more rubber snakes than squirting pens did he sell? _____

Bonus! How many sales in all does his line chart show? _____

Activities for Fast Finishers: Math © 2010 by Jan Meyer, Scholastic Teaching Resources

Dixie's Diner

Dixie's Diner serves the best breakfasts. Use the numbered grid below to create a bar graph that shows what the customers ordered last Sunday. Be sure to fill in the bars up to the correct number for each item.

SUNDAY'S SALES AT DIXIE'S DINER

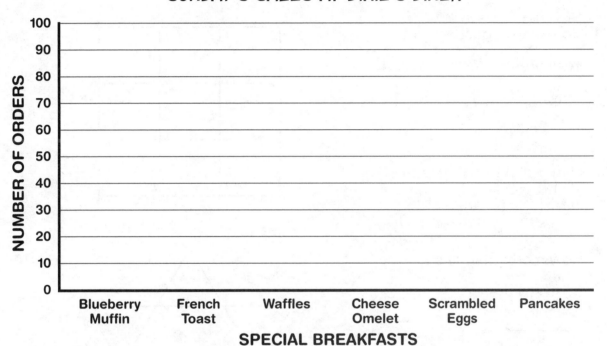

NUMBER OF ORDERS

100
90
80
70
60
50
40
30
20
10
0

| Blueberry Muffin | French Toast | Waffles | Cheese Omelet | Scrambled Eggs | Pancakes |

SPECIAL BREAKFASTS

DISHES SERVED ON SUNDAY	
Special Breakfasts	**Number of Orders**
Blueberry muffin	20 servings
French toast	3 times as many servings as those for blueberry muffins
Waffles	20 more servings than those for French toast
Cheese omelet	40 servings
Scrambled eggs	10 more servings than those for cheese omelets
Pancakes	the number of servings as those for cheese omelets and scrambled eggs combined

Name _____

Date _____

Shape Challenge

How many are there? Count the shapes to find out.

Hint

Sometimes smaller shapes are found within larger ones.

1. How many squares in all are there?

_____

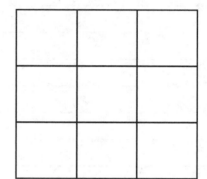

2. How many triangles in all are there?

_____

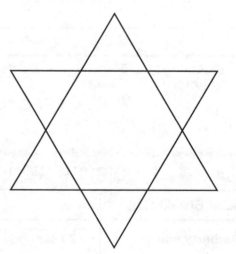

Bonus! Create your own Shape Challenge for a classmate to try. What other geometric shape can you find in this challenge?

_____

Activities for Fast Finishers: Math © 2010 by Jan Meyer, Scholastic Teaching Resources

Name _____

Date _____

Shapely Creation

Create a design in the space below. When you have finished drawing the shapes, add any decorative touches that you would like. Your design should include these shapes:

3 triangles   2 circles   4 rectangles   2 squares

Bonus! For an added challenge, put an octagon somewhere in your creation.

A Math Laugh

Draw a circle around the answer to each of these questions to find the answer to a silly riddle.

Length

1. Which of these is the most likely measurement for the height of a door?

     c. 3 feet   **d.** 50 feet   **e.** 7 feet

2. Which of these should be used to measure the height of a building?

     a. feet   **b.** inches   **c.** miles

3. Which of these is the most likely height of a giraffe?

     h. 15 inches   **i.** 15 feet   **j.** 15 yards

Capacity

4. Which of these should be used to measure the amount of water in a swimming pool?

     b. quarts   **c.** gallons   **d.** ounces

5. Which of these is the smallest unit of measurement

     c. gallon   **d.** pint   **e.** quart

6. Which of these is the most likely amount in a glass of milk?

     p. 25 cups   **q.** 1 quart   **r.** 8 ounces

Weight

7. Which of these has a weight that should be measured in pounds?

     s. a feather   **t.** a human baby   **u.** a grape

8. Which of these is the most likely weight of an elephant?

     q. 4 pounds   **r.** 4 tons   **s.** 4 ounces

Write the letters of the answers you chose on the lines above the numbers for the questions.

How do you charge a battery?

With a C ___ ___ ___ ___   ___ ___ ___ D
      6   1   5   3   7   4   2   8

Name _____

Date _____

Measurement Match-Ups

Draw a line from a measurement in the left column to a measurement in the right column that is equal in length.

MEASUREMENTS OF LENGTH

12 inches = 1 foot
36 inches = 1 yard
3 feet = 1 yard

1. 24 inches	**a.** 6 inches
2. 6 feet	**b.** 4 yards
3. 18 inches	**c.** 9 feet
4. 36 inches	**d.** 2 feet
5. 12 feet	**e.** 4 feet
6. 60 inches	**f.** ⅓ foot
7. 4 inches	**g.** 1½ feet
8. 3 yards	**h.** 2 yards
9. 48 inches	**i.** 5 feet
10. ½ foot	**j.** 1 yard

• A Silly Riddle •

How many feet are in a yard?

Answer: That depends on how many people are standing in it.

Name _____

Date _____

Mr. Knapp's Rug Shop

Mr. Knapp's rugs are too plain! Follow the directions below and help him by making his rugs much more attractive.

- Draw flowers on the rug with a perimeter of 26 feet.
- Draw stripes on the rug with a perimeter of 20 feet.
- Draw a smiling face in the center of the rug with an area of 36 feet.
- Draw a design of your choice on the rug with an area of 15 feet.

PERIMETER AND AREA

The **perimeter** is the distance around a figure. To find the perimeter, add together the length of the two sides and the width of the two sides. The **area** of a figure is the number of square units inside a figure. The area of a figure can be found by multiplying the length times the width.

A

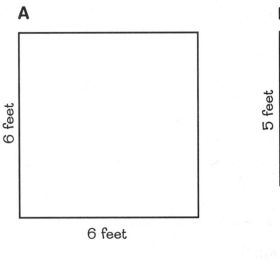

6 feet

6 feet

B

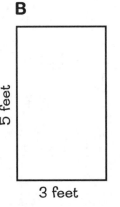

5 feet

3 feet

C

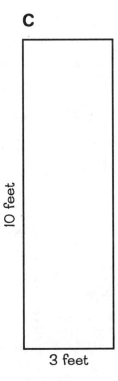

10 feet

3 feet

D

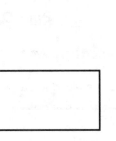

2 feet

8 feet

Time for a Laugh

Draw a circle around your answer to each of these questions to find the answer to a silly riddle.

1. Shelby's tap lesson started at 9:45 and ended at 10:30. How long was the it?

   r. 30 minutes   **s.** 45 minutes   **t.** 60 minutes

2. The movie ran 90 minutes. If it ended at 3:00, what time did it begin?

   s. 1:00   **t.** 1:30   **u.** 2:30

3. Ricky has had his new puppy for four weeks. How many days is that?

   k. 24 days   **l.** 21 days   **m.** 28 days

4. Yoko's fastest time in the skating race was 75 seconds. Becky's fastest time was 1 ½ minutes. Who was faster?

   l. Becky   **m.** Yoko

5. Mr. Perry was in Chicago for 2 days. How many hours was he away?

   d. 60 hours   **e.** 48 hours   **f.** 120 hours

6. Lee was eating pizza at the mall from 5:15 until 5:35. How long was that?

   g. 30 minutes   **h.** 20 minutes   **i.** 25 minutes

7. It's 7:30 a.m. Which is it more likely that you are eating?

   f. lunch   **g.** dinner   **h.** breakfast

8. How many hours are there between 12:00 p.m. and 12:00 a.m.?

   a. 12 hours   **b.** 24 hours   **c.** 10 hours

Write the letters of the answers you chose on the lines above the numbers of each of the questions.

How do you divide 5 potatoes evenly among 3 people?

___ ___ ___ ___   ___ ___ ___ ___
 4   8   1   7   2   6   5   3

It's About Time!

Mr. and Mrs. Bumble think it's a perfect day to go to the beach. They want to be there in time to enjoy a picnic lunch. Answer each question by drawing hands in the correct position on the nearby clock face.

1. The Bumbles' car pulled out of the driveway at 10:15. Just 15 minutes later Billy Bumble said, "I've forgotten my swim fins." Mr. Bumble sighed and turned the car around. What time was it then?

2. They set off again. At 11:05 Betsy Bumble realized that she had forgotten to feed the cat. It took 20 minutes to get back home. What time was it then?

3. Once again they were on their way to the beach. At 12:30 Mr. Bumble pulled off the road because the car had a flat tire. It took 30 minutes to get back on the road. What time was it then?

4. By then, everyone was really hungry. "Let's stop at the next rest stop," said Mrs. Bumble. "We can sit and eat our picnic lunch there." They reached the rest stop at 1:15 and stayed there for 45 minutes. What time was it then?

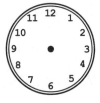

5. At 2:10, Mrs. Bumble realized that she had left her sunglasses at the rest stop. It took 10 minutes to get back to the rest stop. What time was it then?

6. After they left the rest stop, they reached the turnoff at 3:45. The Bumbles finally arrived at the beach 30 minutes later. What time was it then?

Activities for Fast Finishers: Math © 2010 by Jan Meyer, Scholastic Teaching Resources

The Shiver Shop

Wilma Witch has gone to the Shiver Shop to buy ingredients for her magic spells. Help her figure out how much the items that she wants will cost.

1. Beetle wings cost a dime each. How many can Wilma buy for one dollar? _____

2. A small bag of slimy snails costs 25¢ and a cup of snail ooze costs 40¢. How much must she pay if she buys both? _____

3. One pound of ground bedbugs costs one dollar. How much will half of a pound cost? _____

4. Wilma needs lizard toes. They cost 8¢ each. How much will 11 lizard toes cost? _____

5. How many quarters does she need to buy ten lizard toes? _____

6. Each jar of jellyfish jelly costs a quarter. How many jars can Wilma buy for two dollars? _____

7. If fresh swamp scum costs $1.45 for one pint, how much will two pints cost? _____

Bonus! What is the cost of five pounds of ground bedbugs, four small bags of slimy snails, and 20 beetle wings? _____

Activities for Fast Finishers: Math © 2010 by Jan Meyer, Scholastic Teaching Resources

Name _____

Date _____

Snack-Stand Sums

Everyone's hungry and thirsty at Swim-n-Splash Water Park. You're the cashier at the snack stand there. Read each order. Then fill in the costs and add to find the totals.

popcorn	50¢
cheeseburger	$3.50
lemonade	$1.10
yogurt smoothie	$1.40
pizza slice	$1.25
ice cream	$1.35
hot dog	$1.50
pretzels	45¢
iced tea	$1.00
fruit salad	$1.05
brownie	75¢

1. 2 smoothies _____

   4 popcorns _____

   TOTAL _____

2. 2 cheeseburgers _____

   1 hot dog _____

   1 pretzels _____

   TOTAL _____

3. 3 lemonades _____

   2 iced teas _____

   2 brownies _____

   TOTAL _____

4. 4 fruit salads _____

   2 ice creams _____

   TOTAL _____

5. 2 hot dogs _____

   4 pizza slices _____

   6 lemonades _____

   TOTAL _____

Bonus!

Randy has ordered a cheeseburger and an iced tea. He has $5.25. What one more thing can he order and spend all of his money?

1 cheeseburger	$3.50
1 iced tea	$1.00
1 _____	_____
TOTAL	$5.25

Activities for Fast Finishers: Math © 2010 by Jan Meyer, Scholastic Teaching Resources

Exact Change, Please

Write in the number of coins needed to exactly total the amounts on the left. There are many combinations you might make, but you must pick the **fewest** coins possible.

EXAMPLE: You can make 33¢ with 3 dimes and 3 pennies, but this would take 6 coins. Using a quarter, a nickel, and 3 pennies uses just 5 coins.

	Quarter 25¢	Dime 10¢	Nickel 5¢	Penny 1¢
33¢	_____	_____	_____	_____
85¢	_____	_____	_____	_____
24¢	_____	_____	_____	_____
65¢	_____	_____	_____	_____
$1.16	_____	_____	_____	_____
58¢	_____	_____	_____	_____
$2.05	_____	_____	_____	_____
12¢	_____	_____	_____	_____
$3.25	_____	_____	_____	_____
73¢	_____	_____	_____	_____

Bonus! How many nickels do you need to equal $2.00? _____

Name _____

Date _____

What's in Their Pockets?

1. In one of his pockets Jerome has 2 coins that total 30¢.

What coins does he have? _____ and _____

2. In another pocket he has 3 of the same kind of coin that total 15¢.

Which coin is this? _____

3. In his jacket pocket he has 4 coins that total 13¢.

What coins does he have? _____ ,

_____ , _____ , _____

4. Mandy finds 8 of the same kind of coin in one of her pockets.

She counts $2.00! Which coin is this? _____

5. She has 4 coins that total 17¢ in her skirt pocket.

What coins does she have? _____ ,

_____ , _____ , _____

6. She has 3 coins that total 40¢ in her blouse pocket.

What coins does she have? _____ , _____ ,

_____

COINS

Penny = 1¢   **Nickel = 5¢**   **Dime = 10¢**   **Quarter = 25¢**

Activities for Fast Finishers: Math © 2010 by Jan Meyer, Scholastic Teaching Resources

Name _____

Date _____

MONEY

Money, Money, Money

Follow the chain of clues to find out how much money each of these boys and girls has saved or earned.

These children have been saving money in their special banks.

CLUES	MONEY SAVED
Dino has saved $4.20.	_____
Joy has saved twice as much money as Dino.	_____
Allison has saved $1.00 less than Joy.	_____
Lucas has saved $2.10 more than Allison.	_____
Carlos has saved $1.50 less than Lucas.	_____
Olivia has saved 50¢ less than Carlos.	_____

1. Who has saved the most money? _____

2. Who has saved the smallest amount of money? _____

These children have been raking leaves and walking dogs to earn money.

CLUES	MONEY EARNED
Brian has earned $12.50.	_____
Jason has earned $5.00 less than Brian.	_____
Max has earned as much as Brian and Jason combined.	_____
Debra has earned half as much as Max.	_____
Sasha has earned $8.00 more than Debra.	_____
Beth has earned twice as much as Sasha.	_____

3. Who has earned the most money? _____

4. Who has earned the smallest amount of money? _____

Activities for Fast Finishers: Math © 2010 by Jan Meyer, Scholastic Teaching Resources

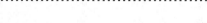

51

Name _____

Date _____

Magic Squares

In these magic squares, fill in the missing numbers so that every row—vertical, horizontal and diagonal—adds up to the sum in the star. Use the numbers in each answer box to help you.

EXAMPLE: ⭐ 18

9	4	5
2	6	10
7	8	3

1. ⭐ 15

		2
	5	
8		6

Answers
1   4   7   9   3

2. ⭐ 12

	4	8
7	2	

Answers
1   5   0   6   3

3. ⭐ 21

	5	6
	7	

Answers
11   4   8   3   10   9

Bonus! ⭐ 18

5	10	
	6	

Name _____

Date _____

Magic Triangles

In these magic triangles, fill in the numbers from the oval next to it, so that each side of the triangle adds up to the same sum.

EXAMPLE:
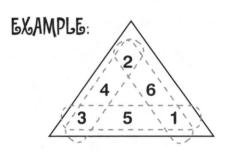

1.
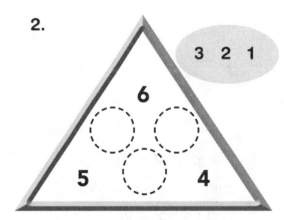

2.

3.
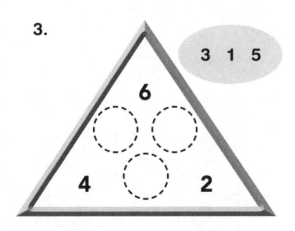

Bonus!
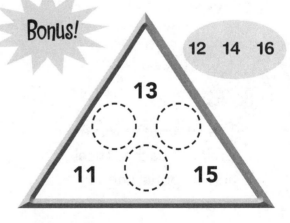

Magic Circles

For each puzzle, use the numbers from the box on the right to fill in the magic circles.

1. The sum of the three circles in each vertical and diagonal line must be 12.

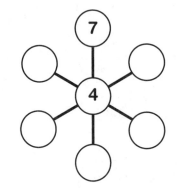

2. The sum of the three circles in each vertical and diagonal line must be 18.

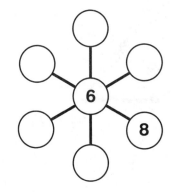

Bonus!

The sum of the three circles in each vertical and diagonal line must be 24.

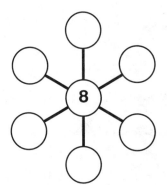

More Magic Shapes

H ere are some more magic shapes to try. Follow the directions to complete each puzzle.

1. Write each of the numbers 1, 2, and 5 once in the boxes at the right so that the numbers in the row across and the column down add up to 9.

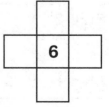

2. Write each of the numbers 1, 3, and 9 once in the boxes at the right so that the numbers in the row across and the column down add up to 15.

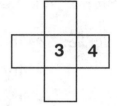

3. Write each of the numbers 3, 4, 6, and 7 once in the boxes at the right so that the numbers in the row across and the column down add up to 15.

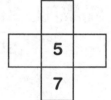

4. Write each of the numbers 2, 3, 5, and 6 once in the boxes at the right so that the numbers in the row across and the column down add up to 12.

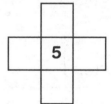

5. Write each of the numbers 2, 4, 8, and 10 once in the boxes at the right so that the numbers in the row across and the column down add up to 18.

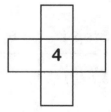

Name _____

Date _____

Do the Two-Step

What's happening to the numbers in the "Step 2" row of each group? Look at the relationship between the "Step 1" numbers and the "Step 2" numbers provided. Then fill in the missing numbers.

Hints:
- Try adding the same number to each "Step 1" number.
- Try subtracting the same number from each "Step 1" number.
- Try multiplying each "Step 1" number by the same number.

EXAMPLE:

Step 1	2	7	14	20	25
Step 2	4	9		22	

In this example, "2" has been added to each of the "Step 1" numbers. The missing numbers are "16" and "27."

Step 1	3	9	15	21	34	42	57	66	73	85
Step 2		14		26			62		78	

Step 1	3	5	6	7	8	9	11	12	14	15
Step 2	6			14	16				28	

Step 1	8	17	24	29	38	43	55	61	82	93
Step 2	14	23		35	44		61			

Step 1	8	11	17	36	42	57	69	78	100	128
Step 2				28	34	49				120

Step 1	3	5	6	7	8	9	15	20	54	100
Step 2	30			70			150			1000

Activities for Fast Finishers: Math © 2010 by Jan Meyer, Scholastic Teaching Resources

Name _____

Date _____

Lady Liberty

How long is the nose on the Statue of Liberty? Follow the steps below to shade in the boxes on the hundred chart to find out.

Shade in . . .

1. all of the numbers with both a 1 and a 3 in them.

2. the number of days in 2 weeks.

3. the number of minutes in an hour plus 4.

4. the first four numbers after 80.

5. a 2-digit number between 10 and 20 whose digits add up to 2.

6. the number of hours in a day plus 3.

7. every number between 40 and 50, except 44, 45, and 46.

8. the number of inches in a foot.

9. the number of days in 3 weeks.

10. a 2-digit number between 10 and 20 whose digits add up to 8.

11. the number of cents in two quarters, plus 4.

12. the number of cents in three quarters, minus 1.

13. a 2-digit number between 30 and 40 whose digits add up to 10.

14. every number ending in zero between 10 and 100.

How long is the nose on the Statue of Liberty?

_____ inches

1	2	3	4	5	6	7	8	9	10
11	12	13	14	15	16	17	18	19	20
21	22	23	24	25	26	27	28	29	30
31	32	33	34	35	36	37	38	39	40
41	42	43	44	45	46	47	48	49	50
51	52	53	54	55	56	57	58	59	60
61	62	63	64	65	66	67	68	69	70
71	72	73	74	75	76	77	78	79	80
81	82	83	84	85	86	87	88	89	90
91	92	93	94	95	96	97	98	99	100

Super Challenge!

The double coconut palm has the biggest and heaviest seed of any tree in the world. Follow the steps below to shade in the boxes on the hundred chart to find out how much a seed from this tree might weigh.

Shade in . . .

1. a 2-digit number between 80 and 90 with digits that add up to 17.

2. one half of 100.

3. all of the numbers with both a 1 and a 4 in them.

4. the number of cents in 4 dimes.

5. the number of cents in 6 nickels and 4 pennies.

6. the number of seconds in a minute minus 1.

7. the sum of 60 plus 30.

8. every number ending in 4 between 50 and 90.

9. a 2-digit number between 60 and 70 whose digits add up to 14.

10. the number 12 doubled.

11. the number with two 4's in it and the number with two 8's in it.

12. the difference between 30 and 3.

13. the two numbers between 41 and 44.

14. the number of days in March and the number of days in April.

15. the two numbers ending in 7 between 70 and 90.

16. the number of toes on two feet plus 1.

17. the two numbers directly after 17.

18. the number of months in a year minus 1.

1	2	3	4	5	6	7	8	9	10
11	12	13	14	15	16	17	18	19	20
21	22	23	24	25	26	27	28	29	30
31	32	33	34	35	36	37	38	39	40
41	42	43	44	45	46	47	48	49	50
51	52	53	54	55	56	57	58	59	60
61	62	63	64	65	66	67	68	69	70
71	72	73	74	75	76	77	78	79	80
81	82	83	84	85	86	87	88	89	90
91	92	93	94	95	96	97	98	99	100

The seed of a double coconut palm might weigh _____ pounds.

Activities for Fast Finishers: Math © 2010 by Jan Meyer, Scholastic Teaching Resources

Name _____

Date _____

Math – a – Magic

Learn these math tricks and then amaze your friends with them. First try doing each of these tricks on a separate sheet of paper.

First Trick

a. Pick a number between 1 and 10.

b. Multiply that number by 2.

c. Add 10 to this new number.

d. Divide that number by 2.

e. Now subtract the number you picked from this sum.

My answer is

_____

No matter what number is started with, the answer will always be 5. Dazzle your friends with this trick by predicting that their answer will be 5.

Second Trick

a. Pick a number between 1 and 100.

b. Add 5 to this number.

c. Add 2 to the new number.

d. Next, subtract 3 from this sum.

e. Finally, subtract the number you picked from the results of Step d.

My answer is

_____

No matter what number is started with, the answer will always be 4. Amaze your friends at the end of performing this trick by showing them a scrap of paper on which you had written the number 4.

Bonus Trick!

a. Write down your phone number without the area code or any dashes.

b. Arrange the digits of the phone number to make the largest possible number.

c. Now arrange the digits to make the smallest possible number.

d. Subtract the smaller number from the larger number.

e. Add up the digits in the result.

f. Finally, add the two digits in this result.

My answer is

_____

The answer will always be 9. Isn't that magical?

Name _____

Date _____

Sudoku

Get in on the fun of one of the world's most popular number puzzles! The numbers 1 through 4 go in each row and in each column. The numbers can't be repeated in any row or column. Fill in the missing numbers in the puzzles below.

EXAMPLE:

4	3	1	2
1	4	2	3
3	2	4	1
2	1	3	4

a.

	1	2	3
3		1	
	4		2
2	3	4	

b.

1		2	
	2	3	1
	1	4	
	4		3

c.

2	1	4	
4			2
1			4
	4	2	

d.

1	2		3
	4		
	1	3	
		1	2

TIP

Begin in a row or column in which only one number is missing.

If you have a row in which two boxes are missing numbers, figure out which two numbers are missing in the row.

Then look above and/or below to see which numbers won't repeat.

If you have a column in which two boxes are missing numbers, figure out which two numbers are missing in the column.

Then look to the right and/or the left to see which numbers won't be repeats.

ANSWERS

Page 6
1. 18, 30, 42, 51, 57
2. 81, 75, 67, 59, 51
3. 75, 65, 40, 35, 15
4. 79, 87, 99, 101, 111

Page 7
1. 16, 20, 24, 28, 36
2. 12, 30, 36, 48, 54
3. 7, 28, 35, 42, 63
4. 18, 36, 54, 63, 81, 90
5. 8, 32, 40, 48, 64

Page 8
1. CDE, EFG
2. 26, 55
3. ✖, ▲▲▲▲
4. 66, 44
5. k, o
6. ➔, ↑
7. x, t, p
8. B, W, F
BONUS! Answers will vary.

Page 9
1. 200
2. 400,000
3. 5
4. 45
5. 30 – 8 = 22
6. 11 + 8 = 19
BONUS! a. 22, b. 15

Page 10
1. 30
2. 20,300
3. 5,000
4. 50,100

Page 11

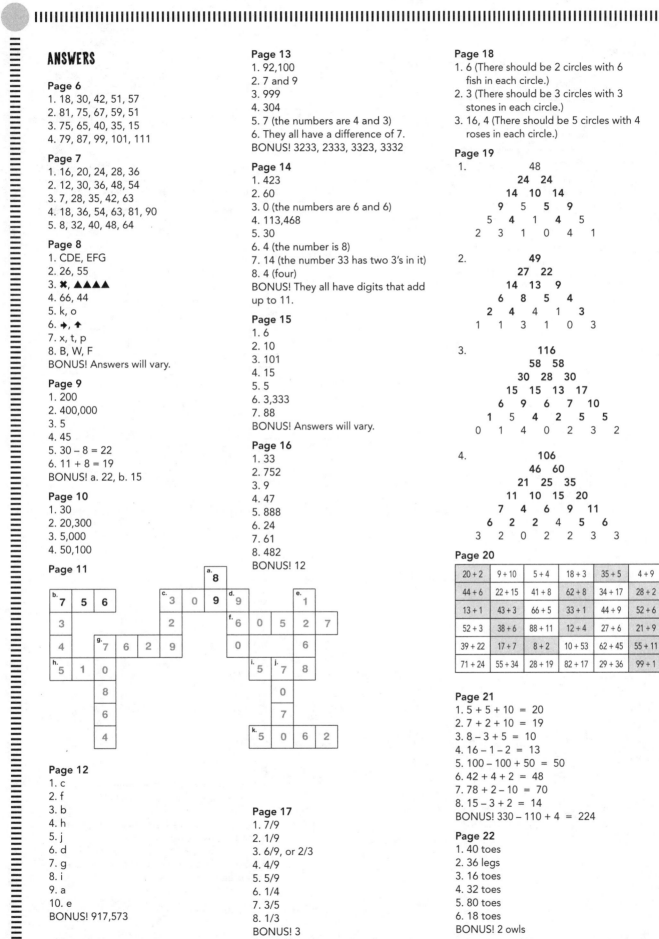

Page 12
1. c
2. f
3. b
4. h
5. j
6. d
7. g
8. i
9. a
10. e
BONUS! 917,573

Page 13
1. 92,100
2. 7 and 9
3. 999
4. 304
5. 7 (the numbers are 4 and 3)
6. They all have a difference of 7.
BONUS! 3233, 2333, 3323, 3332

Page 14
1. 423
2. 60
3. 0 (the numbers are 6 and 6)
4. 113,468
5. 30
6. 4 (the number is 8)
7. 14 (the number 33 has two 3's in it)
8. 4 (four)
BONUS! They all have digits that add up to 11.

Page 15
1. 6
2. 10
3. 101
4. 15
5. 5
6. 3,333
7. 88
BONUS! Answers will vary.

Page 16
1. 33
2. 752
3. 9
4. 47
5. 888
6. 24
7. 61
8. 482
BONUS! 12

Page 17
1. 7/9
2. 1/9
3. 6/9, or 2/3
4. 4/9
5. 5/9
6. 1/4
7. 3/5
8. 1/3
BONUS! 3

Page 18
1. 6 (There should be 2 circles with 6 fish in each circle.)
2. 3 (There should be 3 circles with 3 stones in each circle.)
3. 16, 4 (There should be 5 circles with 4 roses in each circle.)

Page 19
1.
```
           48
        24   24
      14  10  14
     9   5   5   9
    5   4   1   4   5
   2   3   1   0   4   1
```
2.
```
           49
        27   22
      14  13   9
     6   8   5   4
    2   4   4   1   3
   1   1   3   1   0   3
```
3.
```
          116
        58   58
      30  28  30
     15  15  13  17
    6   9   6   7   10
   0   1   4   0   2   3   2
```
4.
```
          106
        46   60
      21  25  35
     11  10  15  20
    7   4   6   9   11
   6   2   2   4   5   6
  3   2   0   2   2   3   3
```

Page 20

20 + 2	9 + 10	5 + 4	18 + 3	35 + 5	4 + 9
44 + 6	22 + 15	41 + 8	62 + 8	34 + 17	28 + 2
13 + 1	43 + 3	66 + 5	33 + 1	44 + 9	52 + 6
52 + 3	38 + 6	88 + 11	12 + 4	27 + 6	21 + 9
39 + 22	17 + 7	8 + 2	10 + 53	62 + 45	55 + 11
71 + 24	55 + 34	28 + 19	82 + 17	29 + 36	99 + 1

Page 21
1. 5 + 5 + 10 = 20
2. 7 + 2 + 10 = 19
3. 8 – 3 + 5 = 10
4. 16 – 1 – 2 = 13
5. 100 – 100 + 50 = 50
6. 42 + 4 + 2 = 48
7. 78 + 2 – 10 = 70
8. 15 – 3 + 2 = 14
BONUS! 330 – 110 + 4 = 224

Page 22
1. 40 toes
2. 36 legs
3. 16 toes
4. 32 toes
5. 80 toes
6. 18 toes
BONUS! 2 owls

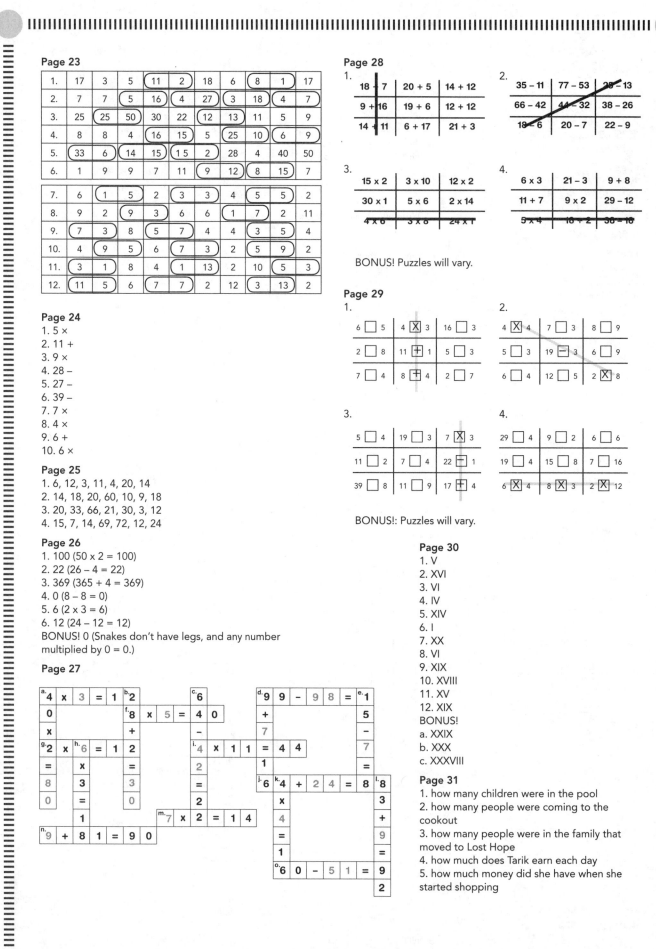

Page 23

1.	17	3	5	11	2	18	6	8	1	17
2.	7	7	5	16	4	27	3	18	4	7
3.	25	25	50	30	22	12	13	11	5	9
4.	8	8	4	16	15	5	25	10	6	9
5.	33	6	14	15	15	2	28	4	40	50
6.	1	9	9	7	11	9	12	8	15	7

7.	6	1	5	2	3	3	4	5	5	2
8.	9	2	9	3	6	6	1	7	2	11
9.	7	3	8	5	7	4	4	3	5	4
10.	4	9	5	6	7	3	2	5	9	2
11.	3	1	8	4	1	13	2	10	5	3
12.	11	5	6	7	7	2	12	3	13	2

Page 24

1. 5 ×
2. 11 +
3. 9 ×
4. 28 –
5. 27 –
6. 39 –
7. 7 ×
8. 4 ×
9. 6 +
10. 6 ×

Page 25

1. 6, 12, 3, 11, 4, 20, 14
2. 14, 18, 20, 60, 10, 9, 18
3. 20, 33, 66, 21, 30, 3, 12
4. 15, 7, 14, 69, 72, 12, 24

Page 26

1. 100 (50 x 2 = 100)
2. 22 (26 – 4 = 22)
3. 369 (365 + 4 = 369)
4. 0 (8 – 8 = 0)
5. 6 (2 x 3 = 6)
6. 12 (24 – 12 = 12)
BONUS! 0 (Snakes don't have legs, and any number multiplied by 0 = 0.)

Page 27

a. 4 x 3 = 12
f. 8 x 5 = 40
g. 2 x 6 = 12
d. 99 – 98 = 1
i. 4 x 11 = 44
j./k. 64 + 24 = 88
m. 7 x 2 = 14
n. 9 + 81 = 90
o. 60 – 51 = 9

Page 28

1.

18 ÷ 7	20 + 5	14 + 12
9 + 16	19 + 6	12 + 12
14 + 11	6 + 17	21 + 3

2.

35 – 11	77 – 53	26 – 13
66 – 42	44 – 32	38 – 26
18 – 6	20 – 7	22 – 9

3.

15 x 2	3 x 10	12 x 2
30 x 1	5 x 6	2 x 14
4 x 6	3 x 8	24 x 1

4.

6 x 3	21 – 3	9 + 8
11 + 7	9 x 2	29 – 12
5 x 4	18 + 2	36 – 18

BONUS! Puzzles will vary.

Page 29

1.

6 ☐ 5	4 ☒ 3	16 ☐ 3
2 ☐ 8	11 ⊞ 1	5 ☐ 3
7 ☐ 4	8 ⊞ 4	2 ☐ 7

2.

4 ☒ 4	7 ☐ 3	8 ☐ 9
5 ☐ 3	19 ⊟ 3	6 ☐ 9
6 ☐ 4	12 ☐ 5	2 ☒ 8

3.

5 ☐ 4	19 ☐ 3	7 ☒ 3
11 ☐ 2	7 ☐ 4	22 ⊟ 1
39 ☐ 8	11 ☐ 9	17 ⊞ 4

4.

29 ☐ 4	9 ☐ 2	6 ☐ 6
19 ☐ 4	15 ☐ 8	7 ☐ 16
6 ☒ 4	8 ☒ 3	2 ☒ 12

BONUS!: Puzzles will vary.

Page 30

1. V
2. XVI
3. VI
4. IV
5. XIV
6. I
7. XX
8. VI
9. XIX
10. XVIII
11. XV
12. XIX
BONUS!
a. XXIX
b. XXX
c. XXXVIII

Page 31

1. how many children were in the pool
2. how many people were coming to the cookout
3. how many people were in the family that moved to Lost Hope
4. how much does Tarik earn each day
5. how much money did she have when she started shopping

Page 32
1. ~~Yesterday, he picked 9 tomatoes and today he picked 3 tomatoes.~~ 20 plants
2. ~~She practices diving for 2 hours each day and always practices 5 days a week.~~ 18 medals
3. ~~Shoji lives 5 miles from his school.~~ 4 miles
4. ~~Each brownie had 4 walnuts in it.~~ 2 brownies
5. ~~On Sunday, the shop rented 70 bikes and made almost $3,000 for the day.~~ $32.00

Page 33
1. what is the difference, subtraction, $6.00
2. have in all, addition, 50 hits
3. how much less, subtraction, 250 pounds
4. what is the total number, addition, 28 animals
BONUS!
Answers will vary.

Page 34
1. 6 marbles (There should be 7 marbles in the third box and 6 marbles in the fourth box.)
2. 3 bracelets (There should be 3 circles with 8 beads in each circle and 6 beads left over.)
3. 30 peanuts (Jake should have 12 peanuts under his name, Gary should have 6 peanuts under his name, and Peter should have 12 peanuts under his name.)

Page 35
Scott has a lizard, Mark has a snake, Zack has a puppy. Carla has a bird.

	Scott	Mark	Zack	Carla
lizard	(yes)	no	no	
puppy		no	(yes)	
snake		(yes)	no	
bird				yes

Page 36
1. nutty double fudge
2. vanilla
3. 20 pints
4. raspberry ripple and mint chip
5. 22 pints
6. 2 pints
7. 100 pints
8. Answers will vary.

Page 37

Player	Total Hits
Gene Rosen	62
Roberto Lopez	78
Matt Branford	52
Montel Clark	69
Steve Williams	86
Vince Nathan	64

1. Steve Williams
2. Montel Clark
3. 15 homeruns
4. 16
5. Steve Williams
6. 26 doubles
BONUS! Matt Branford

Page 38
1. 12 fright wigs
2. wind-up mice
3. squirt pens
4. 40
5. rubber snakes
6. 14
BONUS! 80

Page 39
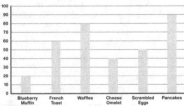
SUNDAY'S SALES AT DIXIE'S DINER

Page 40
1. 14 squares
2. 8 triangles
BONUS! a hexagon

Page 41
Designs will vary.

Page 42
1. e
2. a
3. i
4. c
5. e
6. r
7. t
8. r
Riddle answer: credit card

Page 43
1. d
2. h
3. g
4. j
5. b
6. i
7. f
8. c
9. e
10. a

Page 44
A. The 6' x 6' rug has a smiling face in the center.
B. The 5' x 3' rug has a design of student's choosing.
C. The 10' x 3' rug has flowers.
D. The 8' x 2' rug has stripes.

Page 45
1. s   2. t
3. m   4. m
5. e   6. h
7. h   8. a
Riddle answer: mash them

Page 46
1. 10:30   2. 11:25   3. 1:00

4. 2:00   5. 2:20   6. 4:15

Page 47
1. 10 beetle wings
2. 65¢
3. 50¢
4. 88¢
5. 4 quarters
6. 8 jars
7. $2.90
BONUS! $8.00

Page 48
1. $2.80, $2.00, $4.80
2. $7.00, $1.50, 45¢, $8.95
3. $3.30, $2.00, $1.50, $6.80
4. $4.20, $2.70, $6.90
5. $3.00, $5.00, $6.60, $14.60
BONUS! 1 brownie 75¢

Page 49

	Quarter 25¢	Dime 10¢	Nickel 5¢	Penny 1¢
33¢	1		1	3
85¢	3	1		
24¢		2		4
65¢	2	1	1	
$1.16	4	1	1	1
58¢	2		1	3
$2.05	8		1	
12¢		1		2
$3.25	13			
73¢	2	2		3

BONUS! 40

Page 50
1. a quarter and a nickel
2. a nickel
3. a dime, a penny, a penny, a penny
4. a quarter
5. a dime, a nickel, a penny, a penny
6. a quarter, a dime, a nickel

Page 51
MONEY SAVED
$4.20
$8.40
$7.40
$9.50
$8.00
$7.50
1. Lucas
2. Dino
MONEY EARNED
$12.50
$7.50
$20.00
$10.00
$18.00
$36.00
3. Beth
4. Jason

Page 52
1.

4	9	2
3	5	7
8	1	6

2.

5	6	1
0	4	8
7	2	3

3.

10	5	6
3	7	11
8	9	4

BONUS!

5	10	3
4	6	8
9	2	7

Page 53
1. 2.

3. BONUS!

Page 54
1. 2.

BONUS!

Page 55

1.
2.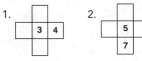
3.

4.
5.

Page 56

Step 1	3	9	15	21	34	42	57	66	73	85
Step 2	8	14	20	26	39	47	62	71	78	90

Step 1	3	5	6	7	8	9	11	12	14	15
Step 2	6	10	12	14	16	18	22	24	28	30

Step 1	8	17	24	29	38	43	55	61	82	93
Step 2	14	23	30	35	44	49	61	67	88	99

Step 1	8	11	17	36	42	57	69	78	100	128
Step 2	0	3	9	28	34	49	61	70	92	120

Step 1	3	5	6	7	8	9	15	20	54	100
Step 2	30	50	60	70	80	90	150	200	540	1000

Page 57
54 inches

1	2	3	4	5	6	7	8	9	10
11	12	13	14	15	16	17	18	19	20
21	22	23	24	25	26	27	28	29	30
31	32	33	34	35	36	37	38	39	40
41	42	43	44	45	46	47	48	49	50
51	52	53	54	55	56	57	58	59	60
61	62	63	64	65	66	67	68	69	70
71	72	73	74	75	76	77	78	79	80
81	82	83	84	85	86	87	88	89	90
91	92	93	94	95	96	97	98	99	100

Page 58
42 pounds

1	2	3	4	5	6	7	8	9	10
11	12	13	14	15	16	17	18	19	20
21	22	23	24	25	26	27	28	29	30
31	32	33	34	35	36	37	38	39	40
41	42	43	44	45	46	47	48	49	50
51	52	53	54	55	56	57	58	59	60
61	62	63	64	65	66	67	68	69	70
71	72	73	74	75	76	77	78	79	80
81	82	83	84	85	86	87	88	89	90
91	92	93	94	95	96	97	98	99	100

Page 59
First trick: 5
Second trick: 4
BONUS TRICK: 9

Page 60
a.
4 1 2 3
3 2 1 4
1 4 3 2
2 3 4 1

b.
1 3 2 4
4 2 3 1
3 1 4 2
2 4 1 3

c.
2 1 4 3
4 3 1 2
1 2 3 4
3 4 2 1

d.
1 2 4 3
3 4 1 2
2 1 3 4
4 3 1 2